HOW TO BE AN

Ocean Scientist
in Your Own Home

OTHER BOOKS BY SEYMOUR SIMON

HOW TO BE AN

Ocean Scientist in Your Own Home

BY SEYMOUR SIMON

ILLUSTRATED BY DAVID A. CARTER

HarperCollins*Publishers*

Library of Congress Cataloging-in-Publication Data
Simon, Seymour.
　　How to be an ocean scientist in your own home.

　　Bibliography: p.
　　Includes index.
　　Summary: A collection of experiments, using easily
available, relatively inexpensive materials, designed
to reveal the various characteristics of the oceans
and the plants and animals that live in them.
　　1. Oceanography—Experiments—Juvenile literature.
[1. Oceanography—Experiments.   2. Experiments]
I. Carter, David A., ill.   II. Title.
GC21.5.S56   1988　　　551.46′007′8　　　87-45988
ISBN 0-397-32291-7
ISBN 0-397-32292-5 (lib. bdg.)

CONTENTS

HOW TO BE AN

Ocean Scientist
in Your Own Home

INTRODUCTION

Imagine yourself in a strange ship slowly drifting downward along a steep cliff tens of thousands of feet high. Your ship has thick steel walls to protect you from being crushed by the enormous pressure of the dark, murky surroundings. Your instruments show that a huge mountain chain with active volcanoes stretches off into the distance. Searchlights on your ship let you catch glimpses of eerie life forms, some with many waving tentacles, others with needle-sharp teeth in large mouths nearly as big as their bodies.

Is this a description of an imaginary planet in some science-fiction story? Not at all. The planet is one you know well. Perhaps it should have been called Oceanus, because three quarters of its surface is covered by water. But the ancients called the planet Earth, and that is how we know it today. The place described above is the depths of the Atlantic Ocean. And the ship is a deep-diving bathyscaphe that scientists use to explore the underwater world of the sea.

Earth's oceans contain over 300 million cubic miles of seawater. So vast are the oceans that if the surface of the planet were made level, seawater would cover the entire world to a depth of 8,000 feet.

Even as space scientists explore our solar system and outer space, so too are ocean scientists exploring the inner world of the seas. Earth is the only planet in our solar system that has an ocean. Yet we know less about our own ocean than we know about the moon, a quarter of a million miles away.

2

We have left footprints on the surface of the moon, yet we have never set foot on the bottom of the deepest parts of the ocean, over 35,000 feet below the waves.

Modern-day science is changing all that. Advanced diving suits permit explorers to descend to depths of 1,500 feet. Beyond that depth, where there is no light and the water presses with a force of as much as 8 tons per square inch, robot submersibles have discovered a great mountain chain larger than the Himalayas and enormous canyons four times deeper than the Grand Canyon. In the black depths of the sea, scientists have found more volcanoes than those we know on land. They have recorded huge landslides covering an area the size of Rhode Island, and undersea storms violent enough to change the underwater landscape but that go completely unnoticed on the surface.

Ocean scientists are interested in the waters of the sea, the waves and the currents, the living things in the sea, and how people can use the sea to make their lives better. These scientists often go out to explore the sea along its margins and in its depths. But ocean scientists also learn about the sea through experiments and investigations in their laboratories. You too can learn about the sea by doing experiments and investigations in your own home.

In this book are many different kinds of projects to help you learn about the oceans and the life in them. Some of the projects are easy; some are more difficult. Choose the ones that interest you the most. Keep a record of what you do and what you discover. You will see that even as you find the answers to your questions, the answers raise new questions. Use this book to help you become an ocean scientist in your own home.

WHAT'S IN SEAWATER?

LET'S FIND OUT: You don't have to live near an ocean shore to get seawater. You can make your own artificial seawater. Here's how: Many pet stores that stock tropical fish and any of the suppliers listed on page 126 carry special salts designed for use in saltwater aquariums. Mix these salts with fresh water following the directions on the package. One pound of the salt makes about 3 gallons of artificial sea-water. You can use artificial seawater in a saltwater aquarium and for any of the experiments in this book that call for seawater.

Of course, you can collect natural seawater if you live near a seashore. Choose places to collect water that are not near sewer outlets or dumping grounds. Often, the farther out from the shore, the cleaner the water. Collect the water in clean plastic containers, taking more than you need so that you will have a reserve supply. At home, store the extra water in a dark place in an extra aquarium or in very clean jars. Make sure that there is no soap or detergent left in the jars when you wash them, and keep all metals away from the water in storage.

HERE'S WHAT YOU WILL NEED: A small amount of seawater or water from a saltwater aquarium; an enamel saucepan; a gas burner in the kitchen; a pot holder; a pair of pliers; a steel sewing needle; fresh water (from the kitchen tap); and table salt.
CAUTION: *Get permission to do this experiment before you proceed. Be careful not to touch the flame or any hot materials.*

HERE'S WHAT TO DO: Pour a small amount of seawater into the enamel saucepan. Place the pan on the burner. Turn on the burner to a medium flame. Wait until most of the water has boiled away. Then turn the flame low and watch the pot carefully. As soon as all the water has evaporated, shut off the flame. Allow the pan to cool down.

How much salt is left? Is seawater mostly salt or water? What does the salt look like? Can you tell by looking at sea salts whether the minerals are the same as in common table salt?

Here's how you can test to see which minerals are present. Moisten one end of the steel needle

salt water

pot holder

saucepan

pliers

needle

table salt

with a little tap water and rub the wet end in the sea salts left in the pan. Light the gas burner and try to get a blue flame, which is the hottest. Using a pot holder and pliers, pick up the needle and place the salty end in the blue flame. Observe the color given off by the heated salt. Do the same thing with ordinary table salt. Compare the differences in color between the two kinds of salt.

Certain substances give off special colors when they are heated. For example, sodium gives off a yellow color. The chemical name for table salt is sodium chloride.

Here are some other substances and their colors when heated: Potassium gives off a violet or light-purple color; calcium gives off an orange-red color; barium, boron, and copper produce a green color. What colors can you see when you heat the sea salts? Because many substances are present in seawater, some of the colors are hidden by others. Scientists use an instrument called a spectroscope to identify the colors they cannot easily see with their eyes alone.

About two thirds of the salt in seawater is sodium chloride. Other substances present are magnesium chloride, sodium sulfate, potassium chloride, and calcium chloride. In the remaining one percent of salts are tiny traces of about forty different elements, including iron, uranium, silver, and gold. (The percentage of gold is so small that you would have to process tons of seawater to get even a tiny amount.)

There are only small quantities of minerals in seawater, but there is so much seawater in the oceans that they add up to a huge amount. It is estimated that each cubic mile of seawater contains over 150 million tons of minerals. And there are over 300 million cubic miles of seawater on Earth. Multiply the two numbers together to get an idea of the vastness of the sea's mineral resources.

You might think that if you added fresh water to the sea salts in the pan you would have the same seawater you started with. That isn't so. Chemical and biological changes take place when you evaporate seawater. Fish and other sea animals will not live for as long in salt water made with evaporated sea salts as they would in natural seawater, because of these changes.

WHEN DOES SEAWATER FREEZE?

LET'S FIND OUT: If you live in a place where the winters are cold, you know that freshwater ponds and small lakes often freeze over solid during a stretch of cold weather. But if you live near an ocean shoreline other than the Arctic or Antarctic, you know that seawater rarely freezes over solid. One

10

reason is that there is much more seawater in the ocean than fresh water in a pond or lake. But there's another reason, which has to do with the differences between seawater and fresh water.

HERE'S WHAT YOU WILL NEED: Several small plastic bags; several rubber bands; a laboratory thermometer (the temperature scale is marked on the glass); fresh (tap) water; seawater or sea salts or plain table salt; the use of a freezer.

HERE'S WHAT TO DO: You are going to find out the freezing point of fresh water and then compare it with the freezing point of seawater. Half fill a plastic bag with some fresh (tap) water. Insert the bulb end of the thermometer into the bag and fasten the bag tightly with a rubber band. Now position the thermometer so that the bulb is in the center of the water.

Place the bag in a freezer. Check the bag every fifteen minutes. As soon as you see ice beginning to form in the water, read and record the temperature shown on the thermometer. Try this several

11

times with several bags of fresh water. Pure fresh water has a freezing point of 0° C (32° F). How closely do your results agree with this?

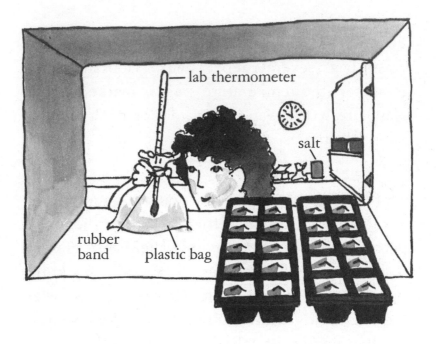

Turn the freezer control to the coldest setting and try the same experiment with seawater in the plastic bag. If you cannot get seawater, try doing the experiment with a teaspoonful of sea salt or regular salt dissolved in a cupful of fresh water. Again, check the bag every fifteen minutes. Record the temperature as soon as the seawater (or salt water) starts to freeze. Compare the freezing point of seawater with that of fresh water.

Salt dissolved in water lowers the freezing point of the water. That's why salt is sometimes scattered on icy roads. The salt begins to dissolve in the thin layer of icy water that covers the ice. This lowers the freezing point of the water that froze. If the air temperature is not cold enough for the salt water to freeze, the ice will melt.

Try the experiment again with twice as much salt dissolved in a cupful of fresh water. Compare the freezing point of the heavily salted water with that of fresh water or less salty water. Does a different amount of salt dissolved in water affect the freezing point?

The percentage of salt dissolved in seawater is called its salinity. The salinity of seawater is not always the same. For example, the salinity of seawater in bays at the mouths of rivers is less than the salinity of seawater in mid ocean. This less salty water is sometimes called brackish water. Do you think the freezing point of all seawater is the same? Why or why not?

Ocean scientists check the salinity of the water and the expected temperatures. Then they try to make a forecast. In the Far North, scientists are often able to accurately predict when the ocean will start to freeze to within a few days. But on the southern fringes of the Arctic Ocean, conditions are much more variable. Here, where most shipping lanes are found, predictions about ice formation are accurate only to a week or two. Can you tell why it is important to know in advance when ice will start to form in northern shipping ports?

HOW CAN YOU MAKE
FRESH WATER FROM SEAWATER?

LET'S FIND OUT: Fresh water isn't found all over planet Earth in equal amounts. Some places have large lakes and lots of fresh water. But other places have little fresh water and get almost no rain. In some areas of Africa, droughts are so severe that crops fail and widespread hunger and famine result.

15

Imagine how wonderful it would be to change some of the ocean waters into fresh water whenever you needed! There is a way to do that.

HERE'S WHAT YOU WILL NEED: A disposable aluminum broiler pan; a heavy piece of cardboard slightly larger than the pan; black paint and a paintbrush; aluminum foil; several wire coat hangers; a roll of plastic food wrap; a glass; and seawater or some other salty water.

HERE'S WHAT TO DO: Paint the inside of the broiler pan black and let it dry completely. Cover the cardboard with aluminum foil and shape up the edges of the foil to form a trough all the way around. Push down the trough at one of the corners to make an outlet at one side.

Place the black pan on the aluminum-covered cardboard inside the trough. Bend the wire hangers into a tentlike shape about the same size as the cardboard. Cover the sides of the tent with the plastic sheeting.

Pour a cupful or two of seawater or salty water into the broiler pan. Place the wire and plastic tent

16

completely over the cardboard (see drawing). Now put the whole model in sunlight or several feet below a heat lamp or strong light bulb. Put the glass beneath the outlet to catch the fresh water you will be making. You have just made a model of a solar distillation plant.

Here's what's happening. The rays of the sun (or light bulb) pass through the plastic sides of the tent. The black color of the pan absorbs the rays and the pan becomes warm. The pan begins to warm the

17

seawater. Some of the seawater evaporates and becomes water vapor. The water vapor is trapped in the plastic tent. It condenses back into water on the inside of the plastic tent. The water drips down the plastic and then into the aluminum trough. After enough water is in the trough, tilt the cardboard slightly so that the water will flow to the outlet and into the glass.

Taste the water in the glass. Is it salty? How does that prove that salt does not evaporate from seawater? How much fresh water can you get using this model in the sun for one hour? Could you use this kind of a solar distillation plant at night? On a cloudy day? In a place where there is not much sunshine? What other energy sources besides the sun or a light bulb could you use to heat the water and make it evaporate?

Making fresh water from seawater is simple. You just heat the seawater and then cool the water vapor. In nature, the sun turns billions of tons of seawater into fresh water every day. The seawater is heated and goes into the air as water vapor. The vapor condenses into the tiny droplets of water that make up clouds. And fresh water falls from the clouds in

18

the form of rain, snow, hail, and sleet. But the rain doesn't fall everywhere. Some places get lots of rain, but other places get almost none.

Distillation is only one of the methods used by people in making fresh water from seawater. Other methods of desalting water include partly freezing the water so that the salt and other impurities are left out; using chemicals to remove the salt; using filters to remove the salt; and even using a kind of salt-eating bacteria.

Already there are more than seven hundred desalting, or desalinization, plants in operation around the world. These plants produce hundreds of millions of gallons of fresh water every day. Some countries in the Middle East produce all or nearly all of the water they need from desalinization plants.

The problem of desalinization is how to do it economically. In 1952, it cost about four dollars to make 1,000 gallons of fresh water from seawater. In 1987, costs ranged down to one dollar or even less per 1,000 gallons of fresh water. And scientists are constantly searching for even less expensive ways to desalt seawater. Plentiful fresh water will benefit all the peoples of the world.

HOW SALTY IS SEAWATER?

LET'S FIND OUT: Ordinary table salt is a mineral called sodium chloride; it is also the most common mineral found in seawater. Sodium chloride has a salty taste, and that's why seawater tastes the way it does. Seawater has many different kinds of minerals dissolved in it, including aluminum, iron, copper,

20

zinc, and even silver and gold. In fact, about 9 million tons of gold are dissolved in all of the world's oceans. Now, if only you could figure out an inexpensive way to get that gold out of the water!

HERE'S WHAT YOU WILL NEED: A test tube and a cork to fit; small weights to fit in test tube; a chunk of plastic clay; a widemouthed jar; a marking crayon; fresh water; and samples of seawater (or any salty water).

HERE'S WHAT TO DO: Fill the widemouthed jar about three-fourths full of fresh water. Put several small weights in the test tube to weigh it down. Push some of the clay down into the test tube to hold the weights in place. Float the test tube in the water in the jar. Add enough weights so that about half or more of the test tube is below the surface. Keep the weights in place with some more clay. Push the cork firmly into the top of the test tube.

Float the test tube again in the water. Use the crayon to mark the water level on the test tube. Take the test tube out of the water and put it aside.

cork
test tube
clay
weights

crayon

widemouthed jar

Spill out the fresh water in the jar and replace it
with seawater (or just mix some salt with the fresh
water). Float the test tube in the seawater (or salty
water). Mark the new water level on the test tube.
The test tube floats higher in the salty water than
in the fresh water. Can you tell why?

Seawater contains more salt than fresh water does.
A glassful of salty water is heavier than an equal-
sized glassful of fresh water. The saltier or heavier
the water, the denser it is. A dense liquid supports

a floating object more easily than a less dense liquid. That's why salty water makes your test tube float higher than it does in fresh water.

The weighted test tube works on the same principle as an instrument called a hydrometer. The saltier or denser the water, the higher a hydrometer will float. Seawater differs in saltiness from place to place. But on the average, seawater in the oceans is about 35 parts per 1,000 salty. That means that 1,000 pounds of seawater is composed of 35 pounds of salt and 965 pounds of water. But in one part of the Red Sea, 6,000 feet below the surface, the water has about 270 pounds of salt in every 1,000 pounds of seawater.

How much salt is in all of the oceans? A staggering amount! If the salt were taken out of all the seawater in the world, it could cover all the land areas on Earth with a layer 500 feet thick.

A saltwater hydrometer is marked in numbers that tell you how salty the water is. The numbers refer to a measure called specific gravity. The specific gravity of seawater is a ratio of the weight of seawater to the weight of an equal volume of fresh water. Fresh water reads 1.000 on a hydrometer.

The average seawater reads about 1.025. A real hydrometer has a very thin glass tube on top. The tube spreads the numbers out and makes it easy for you to read the specific gravity. You can see a hydrometer in use in many saltwater aquariums. The hydrometer is used to make sure that the saltiness of the water stays just right for the sea animals living there.

A CRUSHING
AMOUNT OF PRESSURE

LET'S FIND OUT: Have you ever heard of deep-sea divers getting the "bends"? Divers have to breathe air under pressure when they go underwater. The deeper they go, the greater the pressure of the air they have to breathe. At the higher air pressures needed at greater depths, more nitrogen (a gas in air) dissolves in a diver's blood and body cells. If the diver comes up too fast, the dissolved nitrogen collects as tiny bubbles in his or her blood and joints, causing extreme pain and sometimes even injury or death. This project will help you understand why there is such great pressure deep beneath the sea.

HERE'S WHAT YOU WILL NEED: Two large, empty tin cans, juice-can size; a large nail; a hammer; a block of wood; water; salt; and your kitchen or bathroom sink.

HERE'S WHAT TO DO: Clean two tin cans from which the tops have been removed. Place the first tin can on a block of wood so that you can hammer holes in its side with a nail. Make one hole near the top of the can, another near the middle, and a third near the bottom. Place the second tin can on the block of wood and make four holes equally spaced around the can, near the bottom at about the same height.

Stand the first tin can over the sink and fill it with water. Observe the distance that the water spurts from each of the holes. Water will spurt farther when the pressure is greater. Is the pressure greater at the bottom of the water in the tin can or at the top of the water? What does that tell you about the pressure as the depth of water increases?

Make some salt water and try the same experiment with it. Does the salt water spurt out farther from the same openings than the fresh water? Carefully measure the distance of the spurts with a ruler and compare them. Salt water is heavier than fresh water. How does that help to explain the difference in the distance the salt water spurted?

Take the second can and place it in the sink. Fill it with water and observe the distances the water spurts on all sides. If the water spurts the same distance on each side, what does that tell you about the direction of water pressure?

You can see that water pressure increases with the depth of water in the can. The same is true with the water in a lake or in the sea. In the sea, pressure increases greatly with depth. The rate of increase is about 15 pounds per square inch of pressure for every 30 feet of depth. At 100 feet down, the water pressure is about 50 pounds per square inch.

That means that a scuba diver must get air at about the same pressure as the water surrounding him or her. It is this equal air pressure inside the cells and tissues of his or her body that prevents the diver from being crushed by the pressure of the water.

Some ocean depths are almost 7 miles below the surface of the sea. At these depths, the pressure of the water is more than 8 tons per square inch! Yet some deep-sea animals are able to live even at that pressure. Again, that is because the pressure is the same inside and outside their bodies. These deep-

28

sea animals will usually explode if brought up suddenly to the ocean surface, where the pressure is so much lower.

SUNLIGHT UNDER WATER

LET'S FIND OUT: Even though there might be
bright sunlight above the waves, it is always dark at
the bottom of the oceans. Light disappears slowly
as you dive down. At a depth of about 100 feet,
you cannot see colors. There are no shadows. Dim
light seems to come from all around you rather than
just from above. At a depth of 1,000 feet, it is darker

30

than the darkest night on the surface. This project will help show you how light is affected by the depth of the water.

HERE'S WHAT YOU WILL NEED: One end of a large tin can; friction tape; an eyebolt and two nuts and two washers to fit (try to get the kinds that are rust-resistant); a hammer and a large nail or metal punch; small amounts of black and white enamel paint; a paintbrush; a ruler or tape measure; and a strong cord 50 or more feet long. This is a waterside project.

HERE'S WHAT TO DO: First, use the tape to cover the edges of the tin so that you don't cut yourself. Then draw two lines at right angles through the center of the tin. Paint the tin white and black in quarters (see diagram on page 32). Using the hammer and nail (or the punch), make a hole at the center of the tin. Push the eyebolt through the hole and keep it in place with a nut and a washer on either side of the tin. Tie the cord to the eyebolt. Using the ruler, make a knot in the cord every foot from the tin.

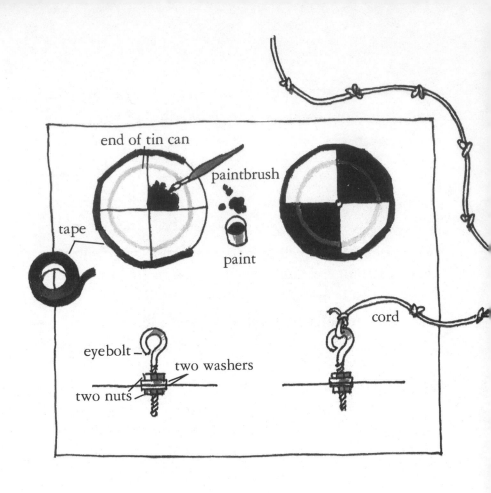

You have made a homemade version of what ocean scientists call a Secchi disc. The Secchi disc helps measure how far light can penetrate under the water. To use the disc, you must go out on a sunny day and lower it into the water from a dock or a boat. Keep count of the number of knots that go into the water. Watch the black-and-white disc until it disappears from view. Record the depth at which this happens. Lower the disc farther and then raise it again until it just appears. Record this depth by counting the number of knots as you raise the disc to the surface. Average the two readings by adding them together and then dividing by two. The number you get tells you the depth in feet to which light that you can see from the surface penetrates the water.

Try the same procedure from a different place or on a different day. You will find that the readings will change from place to place and from one day to another. What do you think would happen if you were to take a reading right after a storm has stirred up the water? Do you think certain kinds of water pollution might change the amount of light penetration? Try taking the light readings in water at different seasons, in fresh water as well as seawater, at dockside and farther out from shore. What other factors might be important?

If you hold a jar of clean seawater or clean fresh water up to the light, the water may look as clear as the glass. The light seems to go right through it. But water is never completely clear. Some light is always being absorbed or reflected by tiny particles in the water. Let's imagine that at a depth of 1 foot only 90 percent of the light gets through. The next foot of water lets through only 90 percent of the remaining light, and so on. By the time a depth of 100 feet is reached, only a tiny fraction of the light gets through. It would be twilight at that depth, even though the sun is shining brightly above. Of course, the amount of light absorbed at a depth of 100 feet will vary depending on the water.

Light is very important for life in the ocean. It supplies the energy used by the tiny plankton plants to make food. It warms the upper waters. Most of the ocean's plants and animals live in the upper levels of the sea, where light can penetrate. There is life in the dark ocean depths. But all deep-sea life depends upon the rain of once-living matter that falls from the levels of light.

WATER TEMPERATURE CHANGES WITH DEPTH

LET'S FIND OUT: If you've ever gone swimming or snorkeling in deep water and dived down below the surface, you've experienced the change in water temperature as you went down. Usually, the water temperature drops as the depth increases, but that is not always true. On very cold days, you may find that the surface water temperature is colder than the temperature of the water at the bottom. That's why in wintry weather, water freezes from the surface down rather than from the bottom up.

HERE'S WHAT YOU WILL NEED: An empty 1-gallon plastic bleach bottle; a cork to fit; a small aquarium thermometer; a short length of nylon thread; aquarium gravel; a small eye screw; a ruler or tape measure; a strong cord 50 or more feet long; and a similar length of thin fishing line. This is a waterside project.

HERE'S WHAT TO DO: Rinse the bleach bottle thoroughly. After the bottle is clean, half fill it with gravel. Attach one end of the nylon thread to the thermometer and the other end to the neck of the bottle. Place the thermometer in the bottle on top of the gravel. Tie the cord around the handle of the bottle. Then, beginning at the top of the bottle, make a knot in the cord at every foot.

Twist the small eye screw into the top of the cork. Attach one end of the fishing line to the eye screw

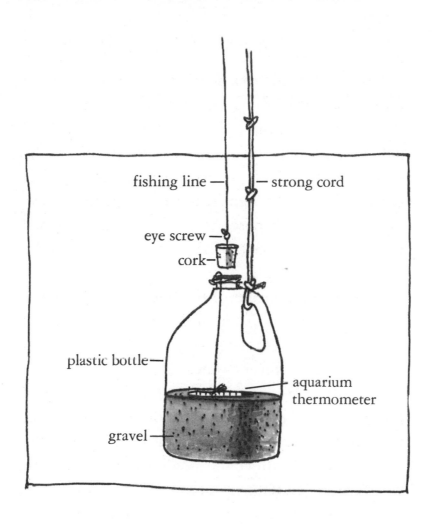

fishing line — — strong cord

eye screw —

cork—

plastic bottle—

— aquarium
thermometer

gravel —

in the cork. Push the cork into the top of the bottle.
You have made an instrument that will help you
measure how water temperature changes with depth.
To try it out, you must lower it into the water of
an ocean or a lake from a dock or a boat.

Lower the bottle to a depth of 5 feet. Lower both the cord and the fishing line at the same time. When the fifth knot on the cord is at the water's surface, pull on the fishing line to remove the cork from the bottle. Wait a minute or two for the water to enter the bottle and the temperature to register on the thermometer, then raise the bottle. Immediately pull the thermometer out of the bottle and read the temperature quickly.

Empty the water out of the bottle and repeat the same procedure at different depths. Keep a record of your findings. Try the same procedure at different places and at different times. Does there seem to be any difference in water temperatures if you take the readings in the morning or the evening? Does the season of the year make any difference? Does the air temperature affect the readings? Which seems to vary more: air temperature or water temperature?

Large bodies of water, such as oceans, heat and cool more slowly than the air or the surrounding land. It may take several months of cold weather for ocean water to cool down in the winter and several months of warm weather for it to warm up in the summer.

Most substances expand when heated and contract when cooled. But water is at its most dense when it is at a temperature of 4° C (39° F). It will expand if it is hotter or cooler than that. That means that the water temperatures at the bottom of a lake during the winter are cooler than the water temperatures close to the surface.

A sudden, very sharp drop in the temperature of ocean water often occurs at depths of from one to several hundred feet. This layer of sharp temperature change is called the thermocline. At even greater depths (several thousand feet down), seawater is icy cold in all of the world's oceans, including those in the tropics around the Equator.

MAKING WAVES
IN THE BATHTUB

LET'S FIND OUT: When you were a small child, playing with water in the bathtub was fun. You quickly learned how to make waves by splashing with your hands. You may have found out how to make monster waves by timing your splashing so that each new splash added to the height of the waves. By the end of your bath, the bathroom floor may have held as much water as the tub. This project will get you back into the bathtub for science—and for fun!

HERE'S WHAT YOU WILL NEED: A small rubber ball or any small floating toy and a bathtub half filled with water.

HERE'S WHAT TO DO: Float the rubber ball (or the toy duck or whatever) at one end of the bathtub. Make waves at the other end of the tub. You can make waves by holding your hand flat just below the surface of the water. Move your hand up and down slowly with an even and steady motion. Try not to splash. You should be able to get a slow and steady wave motion in the water in your tub.

Observe how the ball or the toy moves as the waves pass by. The ball moves only slightly in the wave's direction. Instead, it mainly bobs up and down in a circular motion. The ball's motion shows that the water is not moving along the surface of the water with the waves. The water just moves up and down as the energy of a wave passes by.

Waves are changes in the water that move along the surface. Sometimes waves travel thousands of miles across an ocean. While the waves may move for great distances, the particles of water move only around and around in a circular path.

Water moves in other ways. Currents and tides can carry particles of water along for great distances. Often the currents and tides go in different directions than the waves. For example, you can sometimes see swimmers and small boats being carried away from a shore by an outgoing tide or strong current, even as the waves move toward the shore.

42

As the waves pass by, the boats or the swimmers are lifted up and then let down, just as the ball in your bathtub bobbed up and down.

A knowledge of wave motion, tides, and currents helps sailors ride out high seas without having their boats swamped. Which do you think would be safest: steering a ship alongside waves during a storm or steering through the incoming waves? Try using a toy boat in your bathtub to find out which way is safest before you go out to sea and try it with a real ship.

MAKING WAVES
IN YOUR OWN ROOM

LET'S FIND OUT: If you've ever shaken a sheet or a blanket, you've made waves with each shake. Any one point on the sheet or blanket was only moving back and forth, but the movements were so timed that it looked as if waves were running the length of the material. This project will help you to find out about water waves by experimenting with waves in a stretched rope or a Slinky toy.

HERE'S WHAT YOU WILL NEED: A Slinky toy (a long, coiled metal spring) or a length of rope about 10 or 15 feet long.

HERE'S WHAT TO DO: Fasten one end of the Slinky or the rope to a knob on your dresser or to the back of a chair. Hold the other end in your hand and move about 6 to 10 feet away. Shake your hand up and down slowly to form a moving wave with the Slinky or the rope.

Study the wave as it moves along the Slinky. Notice that while the wave moves forward, each coil only moves up and down. What happens when the wave hits the end of the coil? Does the wave change shape as it moves back and forth?

The high spot on each wave is called a crest, and the low spot is called a trough. The vertical (up-and-down) distance from the crest to the midpoint or undisturbed position is called the height of the wave. The horizontal (side-to-side) distance from one crest to the next is the length of the wave.

Try making higher waves by shaking your hand

a greater distance. Does the height of the wave change
the length of the wave? Try making the waves come
closer together by shaking your hand more rapidly.
What happens to the heights of the waves when you
have many waves passing in a short time?

In large bodies of water such as oceans, waves
most often are caused by winds. Calm winds cause
low waves called ripples. High winds cause high
waves. On windy days, ocean waves of 30 to 40 feet
have often been observed. Even larger waves have
been sighted, sometimes over 80 feet high.

The speed that a wave travels is usually a bit slower than the wind that causes it. The height of a wave in feet is usually less than half the speed of the wind in miles per hour. For example, a 40-mile-per-hour wind will usually make waves that are under 20 feet high.

The largest of all waves are the killer sea waves known as tsunamis. The word *tsunami* is Japanese for "harbor wave." Tsunamis are not caused by the wind. Rather, they are triggered by undersea or coastal earthquakes, deep-sea avalanches, or underwater volcanoes. The sudden jolt is like the whack of a giant paddle that starts the wave.

Out in the middle of an ocean, a tsunami may pass by unnoticed. The height of the wave may be only a few feet and the distance between crests 100 miles. But when the waves come in close to shore, the water comes together and rises to terrifying heights and strikes with tremendous force.

In 1883, an eruption of the Krakatoa volcano in the East Indies caused a tsunami that reached 115 feet in height and killed thirty-six thousand people along the coasts of Java and Sumatra. Nowadays, a tsunami warning system has been set up in Hawaii to alert people if a dangerous wave is on the way.

OBSERVING
WAVES IN AN AQUARIUM

LET'S FIND OUT: Splashing through waves along an ocean beach can be fun, but waves are anything but fun during a storm. During a bad storm, wave swells can reach heights of 20 or 30 feet and batter a shore for hours on end. Beach houses can be pushed around like toys and entire beaches washed

48

away by the surging waters. This project will help you to understand how the waves can do so much damage.

HERE'S WHAT YOU WILL NEED: An aquarium at least 24 inches long; water; some small corks; a spool of strong thread; metal washers or nuts to use as weights; a ruler; some beach sand or aquarium gravel; and a crayon to write on the glass sides of the aquarium.

HERE'S WHAT TO DO: Half fill the aquarium with water. Tie each of the corks to a weight with thread. Use different lengths of thread on each cork so that one cork will float 1 inch from the bottom, another cork 2 inches from the bottom, and so on up to the surface of the water.

Make small waves in the aquarium by slowly moving your hand up and down in the water. Observe what happens to each of the corks as the wave passes by. Notice that the cork floating on top bobs up and down as each wave passes. But the corks floating below the surface will bob up and down only if the wave motion is deep enough to affect them.

Look at each of the corks in turn. Do the waves extend to the bottom of the aquarium? How deep are they? Try increasing or decreasing the size of the waves by moving your hands differently. How does the size of the wave affect the depth that it moves the cork?

Let the water in the aquarium calm down and then draw a line at the water level with a crayon. Tape a ruler vertically along the side of the aquarium. Now make waves and measure their height

and depth on the ruler. Measured from the water line, each wave should be as high as it is deep. Do you find this to be true? Try making different-sized waves and measuring their height and depth again. What happens now? Can you see why a submarine would have to submerge to a greater depth to escape from the high waves of stormy seas?

Does the depth of the water affect how deeply the wave moves? What happens when the waves come to the shoreline, where the water is very shallow? You can place some beach sand in the aquarium and slope it at an angle so that it is like a shore. Now make some small, steady waves.

When a wave approaches shallow water, the trough touches the bottom and begins to slow down. The water at the crest continues at the same speed as before. The front part of the wave becomes steeper and steeper. The crest of the wave loses its support and does a forward roll. The wave forms what is known as a breaker. Waves break when the depth of the water is just a bit more than the wave height.

As a wave breaks along a shore, water is flung high up on the beach. The onrushing water is called a wash. The returning rush of water is called a backwash or undertow. Waves wear away a shoreline by a process called erosion. They also build up the land by a process called deposition. Usually, larger waves cause erosion, while smaller waves deposit material along a shoreline.

Can you see the effect of erosion in your aquarium? What happens to the sand or the gravel being worn away? Try making bigger or smaller waves to see if the size of the waves affects the amount of erosion. If you live near a shoreline, you can see the effects of erosion firsthand. Often, the shoreline will be washed away by the great waves of the winter months and then built back up by the smaller waves of the summer.

HOW WATER TEMPERATURE
AFFECTS OCEAN CURRENTS

LET'S FIND OUT: Water temperature and ocean
currents are not just of scientific interest. They directly influence climate and weather. The air blow-
ing off the warm ocean water of the Gulf Stream
brings mild weather to coastal areas in Europe. For
example, New York is at a latitude of only 100 miles

north of Lisbon, Portugal. But New York has an average January temperature of $-1°$ C ($31°$ F), while Lisbon averages nearly $20°$ F warmer. Colder ocean currents have a reverse effect, bringing cooler temperatures to the western coasts of South America and southern Africa.

HERE'S WHAT YOU WILL NEED: An aquarium or a wide-mouthed glass jar; water; red ink (or a vegetable dye such as food coloring); pepper grains; an ice cube tray; and a freezer.

HERE'S WHAT TO DO: Mix a bit of red ink with water to get a dark-red solution. Fill an ice cube tray with the red water and place it in the freezer. When the red ice cubes are ready, half fill the aquarium or the glass jar with fresh, warm water. Sprinkle some pepper grains on the surface of the water. The motion of the grains will show you the motion of surface water currents.

Place a red ice cube in the water on one side of the aquarium or the jar. As the ice cube melts, you can easily see the motion of the cold (red) water. In what direction does the cold water move? What happens to the cold water as it begins to warm up?

54

What happens to the surface water (watch the pepper grains) as the cold current moves along the bottom?

Empty the aquarium and set it up with some fresh warm water and pepper grains. This time place one ice cube at each end of the aquarium. Observe what happens, as before. What you have made now is a kind of model of Earth's oceans, cold at each end (the Poles) and warm in the middle (the Equator).

As Earth revolves around the sun in its yearlong

ice cubes

pepper

dye

orbit, the waters near the Equator receive the more direct sun rays and become warm. The waters near the Arctic and Antarctic receive only slanting rays of sunlight and are not heated as much. In fact, the Arctic Ocean is frozen over all year long, and the waters around the Antarctic continent are similarly frozen.

Cold water (down to about 4° C, or 39° F) is heavier than warm water. So the heavier colder waters at the Poles sink down and flow along the ocean bottom slowly toward the Equator. These water movements are known as density currents.

When the sun warms the ocean waters at the Equator, the surface water expands very slightly and becomes lighter. The warm-water level at the Equator is actually a few inches higher than the cold-water level at the Poles. The effect of this is that the warm water at the surface runs "downhill" from the Equator toward the Poles.

Of course, other factors such as winds, Earth's rotation, and the water's salinity are important in shaping the paths of ocean currents. But the constant exchange of warm equatorial waters and cold polar waters is one of the most important of ocean movements.

HOW SALINITY
AFFECTS OCEAN CURRENTS

LET'S FIND OUT: The sea is not equally salty all
over. Fresh water from rivers, rainfall, and melting
ice lower the salinity of seawater. The salinity of
ocean water is increased in warm places such as the
Mediterranean Sea, where the water evaporates at
a high rate, leaving the salt behind. Water becomes

heavier as it becomes saltier. As a result, currents of lighter (less salty) water flow along the surface into the Mediterranean and other places where the water is heavier (more salty). Smaller, heavier countercurrents flow beneath the surface in the opposite direction.

HERE'S WHAT YOU WILL NEED: A box of table salt; two different-colored inks or vegetable dyes; a widemouthed jar; two large glasses; and tap water.

HERE'S WHAT TO DO: Dissolve a half teaspoon of salt in a glass of water. Add a few drops of one of the inks or dyes to color the water. Mix well and pour the water into the widemouthed jar. Dissolve several teaspoons of salt in another glassful of water. Color this water with a few drops of the second ink or dye. Mix well. Slowly pour the saltier water into the jar containing the other water.

The percentage of salt in seawater is called its salinity. A glassful of more saline seawater is heavier than an equal-sized glassful of less saline seawater. We say that the more saline seawater is denser.

large glasses

dye

widemouthed jar

table salt

measuring spoons

What happened when you mixed the denser saline water with the less dense water? Did they mix together easily? Which went to the bottom? How could you tell? Leave the jar undisturbed for a few hours and check to see what happens. Are the waters completely mixed? How can you tell?

In some places in the ocean, strong currents sometimes rapidly move the surface water away. In these spots, salty bottom water is constantly rising to the surface. These upward currents are called upwellings.

The rich, mineral-laden waters from the ocean bottom are important to the tiny ocean plants and animals called plankton. Plant plankton drift along in the sea and grow in huge numbers wherever minerals are plentiful. Plant plankton are a very important food for animal plankton and for a vast number of other small sea animals. In turn, these small animals are eaten by larger animals such as fish and other kinds of marine life. These areas of upwellings swarm with large schools of fish. Fleets of fishing ships come to these spots to harvest the abundant sea life.

Sometimes, surface ocean currents can be tracked because they are either more or less saline than the waters around them. During the winter, the saline currents of water spill out of the Mediterranean Sea and move westward into the Atlantic Ocean. Oceanographers have tracked these salty waters as far as 2,000 miles before they mix completely with the waters of the Atlantic Ocean.

WHAT CAUSES
OCEAN CURRENTS?

LET'S FIND OUT: There are 300 million cubic
miles of ocean water, and all of it is moving about.
Ocean currents have been known since ancient times.
Spanish explorers noticed the Gulf Stream around
the West Indies, and as early as the sixteenth century were using the current to aid their boats. By

the nineteenth century, Matthew Maury of the United States Navy was systematically collecting observations of ocean currents. Today we are still charting the currents. This project will help you to explore the causes of ocean currents.

HERE'S WHAT YOU WILL NEED: A large, round, flat glass bowl (such as a flat, heat-proof baking dish); a rotating tray (sometimes called a lazy Susan); ground pepper; a small electric fan; and water.

HERE'S WHAT TO DO: Fill the bowl with water to its widest part. Place the bowl on the rotating tray. Wait till the water stops moving and then sprinkle it with ground pepper. The pepper will make the water currents easier to see.

Position the fan so that it will blow air gently on the water from one side. Slowly spin the tray in a counterclockwise direction. Observe the water currents that develop in the bowl.

Surface ocean currents are created by the steady sweep of very large winds called planetary winds. These winds blow across Earth in large areas called wind belts. The main planetary winds are the prevailing westerlies and the trade winds. There are belts of westerlies and trades both above and below the Equator.

You can see that the wind from the fan makes the water in the bowl move in currents. Observe how the water currents in the bowl bend away from the edges of the bowl just as ocean currents bend away from the land masses that they strike.

The other main influence on the direction of ocean currents is Earth's rotation on its axis. If you rotate

a globe, you can see that the areas along the Equator move at a much faster speed than the areas around the Poles. The differences in speed cause water currents to turn slightly. This is called the Coriolis effect (named after the French scientist who first discussed the effect).

The Coriolis effect can be seen with any body in motion, such as winds and aircraft, as well as ocean currents. You can easily demonstrate the Coriolis effect. Remove the bowl from the rotating tray. Place a sheet of paper on the tray and slowly rotate the tray counterclockwise. Try to draw a straight line in toward the center of the paper while the paper is rotating. The line will curve to the right. In the Northern Hemisphere, ocean currents, air currents, and other moving objects veer to the right. The curve is caused by the Coriolis effect.

Now turn the rotating tray in a clockwise direction. This would be similar to conditions in the Southern Hemisphere. Try drawing a straight line in toward the center. This time the line curves to the left. In the Southern Hemisphere, moving objects veer to the left because of the Coriolis effect.

Replace the bowl of water atop the rotating tray

64

and set up the fan again as before. But this time move the tray in a clockwise direction. This will show you how ocean currents move in the Southern Hemisphere.

Some of the major ocean currents are the Gulf Stream, the Japan Current, and the Equatorial Currents. These are all warm-water currents; they flow from the Equator. For example, the Gulf Stream starts flowing from the Gulf of Mexico, near Florida and Cuba. It moves up along the southeastern coast of the United States and then turns northeast. It crosses the Atlantic Ocean to the British Isles and then continues on to Murmansk, an ice-free Soviet port on the Arctic Circle.

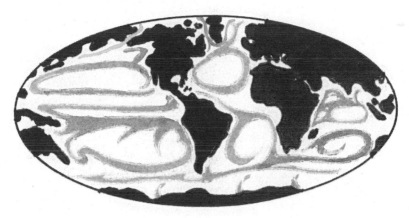

The major cold-water currents are the Labrador, the Antarctic Circumpolar Current (West Wind Drift), the Peru, the California, and the Benguela. Most of these cold-water currents flow toward the Equator. For example, the Labrador Current starts in the Arctic Ocean and flows into the North Atlantic toward Labrador, Newfoundland, and the northeast United States. When the Labrador meets the warm Gulf Stream, the cold waters sink down below the surface and continue toward the Equator.

TIME AND TIDES

LET'S FIND OUT: In most places around the
world, the sea rises and falls twice each day. The
ancient peoples living along the coasts knew that,
and also noticed that the tides came later and later
each day by about 50 minutes. They also must have

noticed that the moon rises about 50 minutes later each day. Since early Greek and Roman times, people have made connections and reasoned that the tides were somehow related to the apparent motion of the moon. But it was not until Isaac Newton published his *Principia* in 1687 that the tides were viewed as one result of the laws of gravitation. This project will help you to understand the connection between the distant moon and the nearby sea.

HERE'S WHAT YOU WILL NEED: A tide table that tells you when high and low tides occur (published in most newspapers and almanacs); a watch; and several hours along a seashore. This is a seaside project.

HERE'S WHAT TO DO: Using a daily tide table, check the times for high tides and low tides on the day that you go to the shore.

Note the time that the highest and lowest tides actually occur at the shore. The waves may make it difficult to tell the exact time, but you should be able to make a good estimate by keeping a close watch. Can you think of what might account for any

difference between the predicted time for a tide and the actual time?

Tides are not like waves. Waves are caused mainly by the winds. But tides are caused by the gravitational pull of the moon and the sun. Because the moon is so much closer than the sun (the sun is about four hundred times farther away than the moon), the moon has a much greater effect on the tides. The moon's gravitational pull lifts the ocean waters in an endless swell that moves around Earth. Unlike surface waves, the swelling tides really move all the water, even at the bottoms of the oceans.

The moon's pull is strongest on the part of Earth nearest to it. The water at that part of Earth moves toward the moon, causing a high tide. At the same time, another high tide is occurring on the opposite side of Earth. This is because the moon is pulling harder on the land closer to it than on the more distant water and pulls the land away from the water. Low tides occur at right angles to the moon's pull, when the moon is either rising or setting. These high and low tides are the daily, or diurnal, tides.

If you look at the drawing, you can see that as Earth rotates, each spot (X) should have two high tides and two low tides every day. The high tides and low tides should follow each other at six-hour (one-quarter-of-a-day) intervals. That would be the case except for one important thing. The moon does not stay in the same position every day. The moon revolves once around Earth approximately every 29½ days. That means that the moon rises about 50 minutes later each day. So each day, the tides

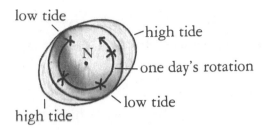

Earth

low tide

high tide

N

one day's rotation

low tide

high tide

Distances and tides not to scale

occur about 50 minutes later than the day before. Check the tide tables to see if that is so.

If the tables indicate the tides are not exactly 50 minutes later each day, here's why: Tides are not simple mechanical things like the gears of a clock. Local conditions such as the shape of the surrounding land and the water depth influence the time of the tides.

The sun also has a small effect on the tides. When the sun and the moon pull together in a straight line (this occurs at the time of the full moon and the new moon), the high tides are very high. These are called spring tides. The word *spring* has nothing to do with the season but is used in the sense of "jump."

When the sun and moon pull at right angles to each other (this occurs at first- and last-quarter moons), the high tides are not so high. These are called neap tides. The word *neap* means "scanty" or "lacking." Can you tell how many spring and neap tides there are each month?

In some places on Earth, there are only small differences between the heights of the high and low tides. But in other places, such as the Bay of Fundy on the east coast of Canada, the tides measure over 50 feet from the high- to the low-water marks. The reason for this is that the Bay of Fundy is at one "corner" of the Atlantic Ocean, if you think of the Atlantic as a four-sided figure. When the tide moves back and forth in the Atlantic, the narrow Bay of Fundy channels the incoming water to a great height. When the water retreats, the level goes far down.

HATCHING AND STUDYING BRINE SHRIMP IN YOUR HOME

LET'S FIND OUT: It may be that the only kind of shrimp you know is the kind that ends up on the dinner table. But the tiny brine shrimp (they're only about ½ inch long when mature) are small relatives of crabs, lobsters, and prawns. The advantage of the brine shrimp for home oceanographers is that they can be easily grown from eggs in a jar. If conditions are just right, you can keep the shrimp alive for about two months—plenty of time to study them. Brine shrimp are also ideal food for goldfish and tropical fish that you may be keeping in an aquarium.

HERE'S WHAT YOU WILL NEED: A small package of brine shrimp eggs (these can be purchased at a pet store that features tropical fish, or see the list of suppliers for aquarium materials on page 126); a widemouthed glass jar or goldfish bowl; seawater or artificial sea salts; a magnifying lens; a thermometer; an aquarium heater; and a package of dry yeast.

HERE'S WHAT TO DO: Dried brine shrimp eggs are sold by the ounce in small containers. A single ounce contains thousands of the tiny eggs, each of which looks like a speck of dust. Brine shrimp eggs will hatch in a few days in almost any kind of salt water, either natural or artificial.

First clean the jar or bowl and then rinse it thoroughly with running water. Do not use any soap or detergents. If you are using sea salts, follow the directions on the package for mixing the salts with water. You can also find directions for water salinity on the brine shrimp container.

You can even use ordinary table salt to hatch brine shrimp. Add about 6 level tablespoons of table salt to about 1 gallon of fresh tap water. (If you have any Epsom salts in the medicine cabinet, add one pinch to the water along with the table salt.) The brine shrimp will hatch in this mixture, but they may not live in it longer than a week or so.

Pour the salt water into the glass jar or bowl and sprinkle a pinch of the brine shrimp eggs on top of the water. The eggs will spread over the surface of the water, and some will sink to the bottom after a while. The eggs that sink are the ones most likely to hatch. Place the bowl in a warm spot in your room (but *not* on top of a radiator). Shrimp will begin to hatch in a day or so.

Once they hatch, brine shrimp will live longer if you keep them in a cooler place. You can even keep them in the crisper section of a refrigerator as long as it doesn't get much colder than 10° C (50° F).

Brine shrimp eggs are commercially gathered from

magnifying glass

brine shrimp eggs

sea salt

goldfish bowl

thermometer

yeast

very salty bodies of water such as the Great Salt Lake in Utah. The eggs are collected in huge clumps, then are dried, packed, and sold in many pet stores in small packages that cost a few dollars. The eggs will hatch in almost any salty water, but they seem to hatch best if the water is a bit more salty than seawater. You can easily do an experiment and add different amounts of salt to water to see what works best.

Temperature is an important factor in determining the length of time it takes the eggs to hatch. If you have an aquarium heater, you can experiment to find out the temperature that is best for hatching the shrimp. Temperatures as high as 32° C or 90° F are not too high for hatching the shrimp. Vary the temperatures in different batches that you are hatching to see which is best.

Baby brine shrimp, called nauplii, are sensitive to light. Place a light at one end of the jar or bowl and see how quickly the nauplii are attracted to it. Use a magnifying lens to study how the nauplii swim and how they behave in the light.

Try to raise the nauplii to adults. This will take about three weeks. After the nauplii hatch, transfer them to a less salty solution such as natural seawater. Make sure they are not too crowded; a dozen or so in a gallon of water is enough. It's helpful, but not absolutely necessary, to aerate the water in the jar or bowl with an aquarium air pump. To feed the growing brine shrimp, mix a package of dry yeast with some warm water. Add a few drops of this mixture to the brine shrimp jar each day.

If you can keep the brine shrimp alive for three

weeks or longer, they will begin to produce young of their own. To study the effects of different temperatures, salinity, light, and other factors, remove a few shrimp at a time and place them in a small jar. In this way, you can do many experiments with brine shrimp without having to hatch a new lot each time.

HOW TO SET UP A SALTWATER
AQUARIUM IN YOUR HOME

LET'S FIND OUT: An aquarium makes it possible
to study the lives and behavior of small sea animals
in your own home. Setting up a saltwater aquarium
and keeping it going is not difficult. You can read
books about it, but the best advice is to begin. You'll
learn more as you go along. Many of the things that

79

seem very difficult when you read about them turn out to be much easier when you do them. The next three projects will provide some hints to help you before you start out.

HERE'S WHAT YOU WILL NEED: An all-glass or all-plastic aquarium of at least 10-gallon capacity; a glass cover for it; an undergravel filter; an air pump; 10 pounds of aquarium gravel—not beach sand— and seawater or chemicals for making seawater. (All of these can be purchased from pet stores that have saltwater supplies or by mail from an aquarium supply house.)

If you live near the ocean and are going to collect seawater, you will need several large plastic bottles or other plastic containers that can be sealed and a filter made of nylon or some other filtering material such as polyester fiber.

HERE'S WHAT TO DO: Clean the aquarium, the undergravel filter, and the gravel with fresh running water. Do not use any soap or detergents, because even a trace of these substances can kill most sea animals. For the same reason, do not use anything

80

made of metal in your aquarium. The metal will corrode quickly, and some will get into the water and poison it. If the aquarium is dirty, use a new kitchen sponge (without soap) to clean the inside and outside. Keep the sponge for use in the aquarium only.

Assemble the undergravel filter according to the directions on the package (it's a very easy job) and place it in the aquarium. It should cover the entire bottom of the tank. A flexible plastic air tube is attached to the filter. The other end of the tube is attached to the air pump.

Cover the filter with 2 or 3 inches of the well-rinsed gravel. When the air pump is in operation, it will draw water into the gravel and then out through the outlet tube. The continuous circulation of water uses the gravel as a filter and will keep the water clean and safe for sea animals. Cover the aquarium with a sheet of plastic or glass to cut down evaporation and keep out dust and dirt.

If you live near the shore or go there on a visit, you can collect natural seawater. Choose a place where the water is clean, away from sewer outlets or dumping grounds. Usually, the farther out from

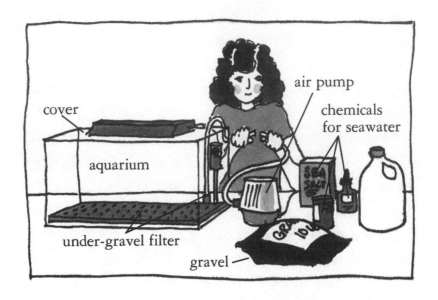

cover

air pump

chemicals
for seawater

aquarium

under-gravel filter

gravel

shore or away from a large city, the better the water. Collect the water in plastic containers, taking more than you will need to fill your aquarium so that you will have a reserve supply. Before placing the water in the aquarium, pour it through a filter made of several layers of clean nylon or polyester to remove particles or dirt.

If you cannot collect natural seawater, you can make artificial seawater that will work just as well.

There are special marine salts that are made just for this purpose. Do not use ordinary salt; use only the kind sold for use in saltwater aquariums. Three pounds of marine salts makes about 10 gallons of seawater. It is usually not a good idea to mix artificial seawater and natural seawater in the same aquarium.

After you pour the water into your aquarium, mark the water level on the outside of the glass with a crayon. Every few days replace the water that has evaporated with clean fresh water, *not* with salt water. You need to use fresh water because water evaporates but the salt does not.

Before placing any marine animals or plants in the water, let the water "age" for at least three weeks. Do not add any materials that you find on a beach such as pieces of driftwood, shells, or sand. These may contain animal or plant matter, which will quickly decay in the aquarium and foul the water. You can tell if the water is fouled by the bad odor it will give off. If the water still smells all right after three weeks, you can begin to add living things to your aquarium (see next chapter).

SEA ANIMALS
IN YOUR AQUARIUM

LET'S FIND OUT: There are many different kinds
of animals you can keep in a small saltwater aquarium, ranging from fish to small crabs, shrimp, ane-
mones, sea stars, snails, and other invertebrates. Don't
try to mix too many kinds together in the same tank.

84

Start out with one or two kinds and see what happens.

HERE'S WHAT YOU WILL NEED: The saltwater aquarium you set up previously (see preceding chapter) and several small sea animals. If you are going to collect sea animals along a shore, you will need a nylon net with a strong handle, several plastic containers with covers, and a face mask and snorkel to let you look underwater more easily. Take along several friends to help you collect.
CAUTION: *Use the face mask and snorkel only when a responsible adult is present.*

HERE'S WHAT TO DO: Observing and collecting sea animals from along a seashore can be very enjoyable, but there are a few things to remember. In some places (all seashore national parks, for example), collecting sea animals may be regulated by federal, state, or local laws. Check before you start out. Also, even if collecting sea animals is not regulated, as a young scientist and a responsible person you should be careful to disturb the environment as little as possible. Collect only what you will use, and be sure that those animals you collect do not belong to endangered species.

Small or young animals that are not fully grown adapt to an aquarium much more easily than large or adult animals. Overcrowding animals in your aquarium is sure to kill even the hardiest kinds. It is much more enjoyable to be able to maintain a few healthy animals for a long time than to have a full tank of sick and dying ones.

When you go out to collect, wear old sneakers and old clothing to protect your legs and feet from getting scraped on rocks or barnacles. For the same reason, it's a good idea to wear work gloves. Take along a net with a strong handle, and perhaps a larger net called a seining net to drag through the water. Take along clean plastic containers to hold your catch. Your friends can help you transfer your catch from the nets into the containers.

Collect shore animals at low tide. Check the newspapers for the times of low tides in your collecting area. The best place to look is in small tidal pools that are left behind when the water goes out. Use your face mask to look below the water. Look in seaweed clumps for small crabs or snails. Look

86

containers

nylon net
tide pool

for small sea stars in mussel or clam beds. If you are lucky, you may find a small sea horse or pipefish among waving strands of eel grass.

Different coastal areas have different kinds of sea life. The kind of seashore (rocky, sandy, or coral) and the water temperature and tides will result in some animals' being abundant in one place but rare in another. Read a local guidebook so that you will know what to expect.

It is very important to remember not to crowd the animals that you collect. Keep the containers out of the sun and as cool as possible. A sudden change from cool water to warm water will promptly kill many kinds of sea animals. One way to keep the containers cool on the trip back home is to wrap the containers with wet rags.

When you get home, do not just dump the animals you have collected into the aquarium. Instead, float the containers in your aquarium for about fifteen minutes until the water temperatures have a chance to adjust. Then slowly tilt the containers and let the waters in the containers and the aquarium mix together. Finally, gently upend the containers and allow the sea animals to enter the aquarium.

Many animals do not live long in an aquarium. Keep a close watch at first to see how your animals adjust. Remove any dead or obviously dying ones at once. If some animals seem to be constantly fighting or bothering one another, remove one of the fighters before both are injured. After a week or two, the remaining animals may have adjusted pretty well. In the next chapter, we'll talk about how to feed them and how to maintain your aquarium in top condition.

If you don't live near the seashore, it is still possible to set up and keep a saltwater aquarium. Supplies and sea animals can be purchased from some local pet stores or through the mail directly from aquarium supply houses (see page 126). Some of these places will sell a hardy collection of several animals for a small aquarium. When you are just beginning to keep a saltwater aquarium, it makes no sense to purchase the more expensive and exotic kinds of saltwater fish. Many are delicate and hard to keep. They need special temperatures and much knowledge on your part. Use your local library or consult some of the books listed on page 128 for more information on saltwater aquariums.

Keeping and maintaining sea animals in a home aquarium will give you a great appreciation of how these animals live and behave. Remember, keeping animals in your home makes you responsible for their lives and well-being.

MAINTAINING A SALTWATER AQUARIUM IN YOUR HOME

LET'S FIND OUT: Once your saltwater aquarium has been in operation for several weeks, everything will become much easier. Even though the aquarium may not look as clean and spotless as a newly prepared tank, the water is probably healthier for the animals. One good check on water quality is the growth of algae (see below) on the sides of the aquarium and on the rocks or coral in the tank. If the algae seem to be growing, then all is well. But if the algae stop growing or the water in the tank begins to smell bad, it's time to replace a few gallons of the water with freshly made salt water.

HERE'S WHAT YOU WILL NEED: The saltwater aquarium that you set up (see pages 79–89); an aquarium thermometer; a hydrometer for seawater; an aquarium dip tube; and various kinds of food for your aquarium animals. All of these are available at many local pet stores or through the mail (see page 126).

HERE'S WHAT TO DO: Use an all-glass aquarium thermometer that can be left in the water. Many of the animals that you collected along the shore can adapt to water temperatures of about 15° to 21° C, or 60° to 70° F. Animals from tropical or subtropical waters need temperatures a bit higher. The important point to remember is to avoid any sudden temperature changes. That means it would be wise to set up your aquarium out of direct sunlight (or at least where it can be shaded) and away from a hot radiator or cold drafts of outside air.

A hydrometer (see page 23) is used to check the salinity of salt water in the aquarium. If the water is natural seawater, keep the salinity at whatever the original reading was. If you are using artificial seawater, keep the reading at 1.025 or a bit lower. When some water evaporates, remember to add fresh water to your aquarium to keep the salinity constant.

Many sea animals can be fed a variety of foods. You can use live brine shrimp (see page 73), raw or boiled shrimp, crab or lobster meat, and almost any kind of lean meat. Cut the food into tiny, bite-sized pieces. It is better to feed too little than too much. Feed once a day, but don't worry if you skip a day or two. Most sea animals can get along without food for several days and even weeks. But don't make a habit of not feeding them. Remove any uneaten scraps of food ten minutes after feeding time. Even the smallest bit of food left in the tank overnight may foul the water.

At first, try a number of different foods to see which ones the animals in your aquarium will eat.

dip tube

thermometer

hydrometer

food

After several days, you will begin to be able to tell which of the foods they eat and which they leave. A varied diet of several different foods is best.

Most sea plants do not do well in saltwater aquariums. Seaweed will usually die and decay and foul the water quickly. The exception to this is the algae that may start growing on the sides of the tank and on the rocks and gravel. Algae may be eaten by some of the animals and are a good addition to their diet. Algae need good light to grow well. But because too much sunlight will warm the water to dangerous levels, it's a good idea to grow the algae in a widemouthed glass jar containing seawater and kept in a sunny location. Transfer the algae that grow in the jar to your aquarium as needed.

If the aquarium water gets too cold during the wintertime, buy a thermostat-heater for your aquarium. This glass-tubed device is sold in most pet stores. Set the thermostat to maintain the temperature you want (this may take a little experimenting), and the heater will go on and off automatically without further adjustment.

If the water gets too hot in the summertime (or if the heater goes on the blink), float a sealed plastic bag containing ice cubes in the aquarium. Keep checking the water temperature and remove the ice pack when necessary.

Animal droppings and other debris should be removed with a dip tube several times a week. (Instructions for using a dip tube come on the package.) It's a good idea to keep an extra supply of seasoned seawater—that is, water that was made several days earlier—in storage in a dark place. Exchange about a gallon or so of your aquarium water with the stored seawater every week or so. Use some of the books listed on page 128 for more information about keep-

94

ing an aquarium. A few minutes of care each day will result in a seawater aquarium with interesting animals that can be maintained in your home for a long time.

WHY DO HEAVY
METAL SHIPS FLOAT?

LET'S FIND OUT: A ship going from the fresh water of a lake or river into the seawater of an ocean will float higher in the ocean than in the lake or river. If you've ever floated in the salt water of an ocean—or in a saltwater pool or lake—you know that it's easier than floating in fresh water. The level to which a ship (or any floating object) submerges in water is called its water line. Why does a ship's or a person's water line change from one kind of water to another? This project will help you find out.

HERE'S WHAT YOU WILL NEED: Aluminum foil; a few paper clips; a widemouthed glass jar; a crayon; sand; a cup or two of table salt or sea salt; an empty aquarium; and water.

HERE'S WHAT TO DO: Fill the aquarium with fresh water to a depth of 5 or 6 inches. Double over a large piece of aluminum foil and bend it into the shape of a boat. Float the boat on the water. Reshape the boat if necessary so that it floats right side up and evenly. One at a time, place two or three paper clips in the aluminum boat. Does the boat still float? Why?

A common mistake that some people make is to think that light objects float and heavy objects sink. You can see that this is not so; if it were true, the aluminum boat would sink with the weight of the paper clips.

97

Take the boat and the paper clips out of the water. Fold the aluminum over, flattening the boat tightly with the paper clips inside. Put it in the water. What happens? Notice that the flattened aluminum displaces less water than the boat.

Can you explain why the flattened foil sinks even though its weight is the same as before? The reason is that any floating object has enough volume (or size) to displace its own weight in water. For a ship to float, the downward force of gravity on it (its weight) must be balanced by the upward force of

water (called buoyancy). How does this help to explain why the aluminum boat floated lower in the water when you added the paper clips?

Take an empty widemouthed jar and push it down into the water in the aquarium. You can feel the buoyancy of the water pushing against your hand. Push the jar deeper into the water and feel how the buoyancy increases the deeper you push.

Take out the jar and pour about ½ inch of sand into it. Place the jar back in the water. Note how deeply the jar floats. You can use a crayon to mark the water level on the outside of the jar. Now pour another ½ inch of sand into the jar and observe what happens. Mark the water level again. When the jar increases in weight with the additional sand, how does its buoyancy change? What happens if a ship adds more weight but its water level is so high up that it can displace no more water?

Take out the jar and add a cup or two of salt to the water in the aquarium. Stir until all the salt is dissolved. Now try the same experiment with the jar and the sand as before. Does the jar float as deeply in the salt water as it did in the fresh water? Can you think of why this is so? It will help your explanation to remember that salt water is heavier than an equal amount of fresh water. Which has more buoyancy: seawater or fresh water?

A seagoing cargo ship can carry more weight than the same ship in a freshwater lake. Can you explain why? How would a ship's water line change when the ship sails from the fresh water of the Great Lakes into the Atlantic Ocean? How does your water line change when you swim in a freshwater lake or pool, and then swim in the salty water of an ocean? In which kind of water would it be easier for you to float?

HOW CAN SUBMARINES
GO UP AND DOWN?

LET'S FIND OUT: The first working model of a
submarine was built in 1620. It was a wooden frame
covered with greased leather. In the Civil War, the
Confederate States produced several submarines for
use in warfare. World Wars I and II demonstrated
the submarine's military effectiveness. Modern-day

nuclear submarines are streamlined vessels that can operate underwater for weeks and even months. Other submersibles, such as Auguste Piccard's bathyscaphe, do deep-sea research. But all submarines and submersibles, from the earliest models to the most advanced, go up and down according to the same principles.

HERE'S WHAT YOU WILL NEED: A tall, narrow jar such as an olive jar; a rubber sheet (a cut-up rubber balloon will do); a heavy rubber band; a medicine dropper; and water.

HERE'S WHAT TO DO: Fill the jar with water to within an inch of the top. Float the medicine dropper in the water, bulb up. Squeeze the bulb slightly and then let it go. The object is to take in just enough water in the bulb so that it barely remains floating. You may have to try this several times to get it just right. Only the smallest tip of the bulb should be floating above the surface.

Now stretch the rubber sheet across the top of the jar and secure it in place with a heavy rubber band. Make sure that the rubber sheet completely seals off the air in the jar. After that is done, press down slightly on the rubber sheet. Watch what happens to the medicine dropper. Release the pressure on the rubber sheet and again watch what happens to the dropper.

If you have set up this demonstration correctly, the medicine dropper will sink down whenever you

press down on the rubber sheet. When you release the pressure on the rubber sheet, the dropper will once again rise to the surface. You can make the dropper go up and down at the touch of your fingers on the rubber sheet.

If the dropper does not sink, take off the rubber sheet and try putting slightly more water into the dropper. It must just barely float on the surface. If the dropper sinks before you press on the rubber sheet, it has too much water in it and you must squeeze some out.

The dropper goes up and down for much the same reason that a submarine can submerge below the waves and then emerge to the surface. To understand why this happens, watch the level of the water in the dropper when it is floating on the surface. Now press the rubber sheet slightly. Notice that the water level in the dropper becomes higher, showing that more water is in the dropper. Why would this cause the dropper to sink?

Pressing down on the rubber sheet squeezes air in the jar and increases the air pressure. The increased air pressure presses down on the water and pushes some of the water into the dropper. The extra water makes the dropper heavier. Because the dropper was barely floating, its weight is now more than its buoyancy, and the dropper sinks to the bottom.

When you release the rubber sheet, the air pressure becomes less. The extra water pushes out of the dropper and the dropper becomes lighter. The lighter dropper rises because its weight is now less than its buoyancy.

A submarine works for much the same reason. Ballast tanks in a submarine are used to make the sub go up and down. When the tanks are opened to the sea, water rushes in, and the submarine becomes heavier. It starts to dive. The submarine goes up again when compressed air, kept aboard in air tanks, is used to push the water out of the ballast tanks. Of course, a submarine, unlike a medicine dropper, uses a motor and diving planes to remain submerged at the desired depth rather than just sinking to the bottom of the sea.

HOW MUCH OF
AN ICEBERG FLOATS?

LET'S FIND OUT: The date was April 14, 1912.
The icy waters of the North Atlantic were filled
with bodies that bobbed up and down in the waves.
Sailors in crowded lifeboats tried to pull people
aboard. Just a short time before, the *Titanic*, the
"safest ship in the world" according to its builders,

had been sailing along majestically. Yet in a few hours, the *Titanic* had gone to the bottom of the ocean after striking a large iceberg. This project will help you to understand why an iceberg may be dangerous to a ship even though it seems a long distance away.

HERE'S WHAT YOU WILL NEED: A plastic bag; a strong rubber band; an aquarium or large bowl; water; and a freezer compartment of a refrigerator.

HERE'S WHAT TO DO: Partly fill the plastic bag with water and close the top off tightly with a rubber band. Place the bag in the freezer for a day or so. After the water in the bag freezes solid, remove the chunk of ice and float it in an aquarium or bowl filled with water.

About how much of the floating ice chunk is above the surface and how much below? The ice is floating in fresh water. How would it float differently in ocean water (see page 22)? About seven eighths of an iceberg floating in ocean water is submerged below the surface. A ship coming near a large iceberg could easily come in contact with the underwater portion while still several hundred yards away from the visible part.

Keep watching the chunk of ice you placed in the aquarium. What happens as it begins to melt? What dangers might occur if a ship were near a large, melting iceberg as it began to turn and shift in the water?

Icebergs are large chunks of ice and snow floating in the oceans. The bergs break away from the ice sheets that reach the sea in polar regions. Here's how a berg breaks away: Seawater melts the ice at the bottom of the ice sheet. The top part of the ice

rubber band ————plastic bag with frozen water

cracks off and falls into the water with a roar.

The giant block of ice bobs up and down. Then it begins to drift away. Some bergs last for years and float for thousands of miles, carried along by ocean currents. Icebergs are often as large as ocean liners. Many are even larger. The tallest berg on record was more than 500 feet above water. That's nearly twice the height of the Statue of Liberty including its base. Can you imagine how deep underwater the iceberg must have been?

Some icebergs are not very high, but are flat and very large. The largest iceberg ever measured was about two hundred miles long and sixty miles wide. That's bigger than the state of Vermont or the country of Belgium.

As a direct result of the sinking of the *Titanic*, an International Ice Patrol was established. Since that time, no more lives have been lost through iceberg collisions in North Atlantic shipping lanes. Iceberg hunts by planes and ships of the United States Coast Guard begin early in March and continue through June or July. The average number of icebergs spotted each year is four hundred, although this can vary widely. Only icebergs near the shipping lanes are carefully watched.

HOW TO SEND
A MESSAGE BY SEA

LET'S FIND OUT: Our knowledge of ocean currents has been built up gradually over the years from thousands of shipboard observations of drifting. Over most of the oceans, the currents are very weak, with speeds of less than 1 mile per hour. In some of the larger currents around the Equator, speeds may be

110

1 or 2 miles per hour. In the strongest currents such as the Gulf Stream, however, speeds may reach as high as 4 or 5 miles per hour. It might be fun to track the currents as Thor Heyerdahl did in 1947 when he sailed on a raft, the *Kon Tiki,* from Peru to the Tuamotu Islands east of Tahiti. That journey of more than 4,000 miles was powered mainly by ocean currents. But there is a much safer and easier way to track ocean currents.

HERE'S WHAT YOU WILL NEED: Postcards; clear plastic soda bottles with screw tops; a wax candle; and dry sand. This is a seaside project.

HERE'S WHAT TO DO: Address the postcards to yourself. On the back of each card, write a short message asking the finder to note the date and the location the bottle was found in and to mail the card. Place an inch or two of dry sand in the bottoms of the bottles to add some weight for ballast. The bottles should float neck down, with only about one quarter of the bottle showing above the water. Roll up the postcards and place one in each bottle. Close the bottles tightly with the screw tops and use some melted candle wax to seal them.

Release the bottles from a ship or ferryboat at some offshore point near the coast. Perhaps you have a friend who will release the bottle at some point more distant from shore. Ask your friend to write down the spot at which the bottles were released.

Each year, thousands of bottles like the ones you

prepared are released by scientists around the world. About one out of ten seem to be returned. From those bottles returned, ocean scientists try to determine the speed and directon of ocean currents. In fact, several scientific organizations offer a reward (usually a dollar) to any finder who will fill out the questionnaire inside the bottle and send it back.

Assuming that your bottles will have about the same rate of return as those of the scientists, you can see that you will have to send out many bottles to get back a few answers. Despite the fact that you will not be able to chart currents with just a few bottles, it should be interesting to find out how far and how long your bottles drift before they are picked up on a beach or at sea.

Perhaps one of your bottles will get a really long ride and wind up across an ocean. Scientists have records of bottles that have crossed the Atlantic from the United States and reached the shores of Great Britain, Ireland, France, or Spain, a distance of about 3,000 miles. Other bottles may make a trip around the Azores and come ashore in the West Indies after a circular journey of 5,000 to 6,000 miles.

How long and how far can bottles travel? The answer is not certain. But in 1929 a German scientist released a bottle in the southern part of the Indian Ocean. It was first reported at Cape Horn at the tip of South America. Dropped back into the sea, it was found in 1935 off the coast of Australia, a journey of over 16,000 miles. Still another bottle released in Australia in 1962 was found near Miami, Florida, five years later.

The record for the bottle in the water for the longest time is probably held by a bottle tossed into the sea in 1784 by a Japanese sailor wrecked on a Pacific island. It is said that, in 1943, more than 150 years later, the bottle was washed up on the shores of Japan, near the village of the sailor's birth.

MAKING A PROFILE
OF THE OCEAN FLOOR

LET'S FIND OUT: Sailors are always concerned
with the shape of the ocean floor as they try to avoid
sailing their ship onto jagged rocks, reefs, and sand-
banks. In old Egyptian wall paintings, sailors are
shown lowering weighted lines over the sides of
boats to measure the depth of the waters. But using

115

a line to measure water depth of a mile or more is not easy. For one thing, currents and surface winds carry the ship far off to one side, giving incorrect readings. Nowadays, scientists use echo sounding to trace the profile of the sea bottom. Another technique, called echo ranging, gives us a picture of large areas of the sea. This project will help show you how echo sounding works.

HERE'S WHAT YOU WILL NEED: A sheet of graph paper, a pencil, and the sounding chart on the following page.

HERE'S WHAT TO DO: The chart below gives the time it takes for a sound pulse to be sent down to the ocean floor and for its echo to return. While the chart does not represent a real section of the ocean, you can use it to see how scientists used soundings to profile the ocean floor.

The speed of sound in ocean water is about 4,800 feet per second. An echo sounder trailed from a ship sends out a series of ultrasonic signals or "pings." When these bounce off the ocean floor, the echo is picked up by a microphone. The time interval be-
116

tween the "ping" and its echo gives a measure of the ocean's depth. Here is a formula you can use with the table to calculate depths:

$$\text{Depth (in feet)} = \frac{\text{Time (in seconds)} \times 4800}{2}$$

Fill in the last column of the chart (on a separate piece of paper) and use the depths you calculated to draw a profile of the ocean floor on a piece of graph paper.

Echo Sounder Chart

Station Number	Horizontal Distance (miles)	Time (seconds)	Depth (feet)
1	0	3.2	7,680
2	10	3.5	(You
3	20	3.9	complete
4	30	4.6	these)
5	40	4.9	
6	50	5.1	↓
7	60	5.0	
8	70	4.3	
9	80	2.2	
10	90	3.4	
11	100	4.2	

Plot these depths on a piece of graph paper. Remember to plot the numbers *downward* because the depths are below sea level. How deep is the deepest point you have plotted? Is there a mountain? Where? Make up your own numbers to simulate how a flat plain or a double mountain would look on an echo sounder.

Of course, scientists nowadays use computers to

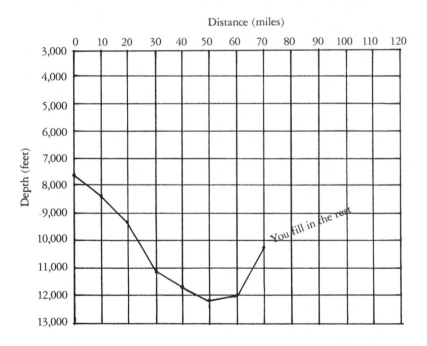

find out these figures and to draw the chart. They also use new techniques of echo ranging that are similar to radar in that they give a three-dimensional picture of the ocean bottom.

At one time, many people thought that the ocean floor was a flat, muddy plain. But now oceanographers know that the ocean floor is a jagged seascape of canyons, valleys, trenches, plains, and mountains. In fact, the deepest places in the ocean are farther beneath the waves than Mount Everest is above sea level. And one enormous undersea mountain chain, the Mid-Oceanic Ridge, about 35,000 miles long, nearly encircles Earth from Pole to Pole.

Close to the continents, the average depth of the ocean bottom is just a few hundred feet. This plateau, known as the continental shelf, slopes gently downward for some 50 miles beyond the edge of the land.

At the outer edge of the shelf, the seafloor drops steeply downward for about another 50 miles. This is called the continental slope. It is the continental slope, not the visible coastline, that marks the true edge of a continent. Beyond the slope lies the deep ocean floor, thousands of feet below the surface of the water.

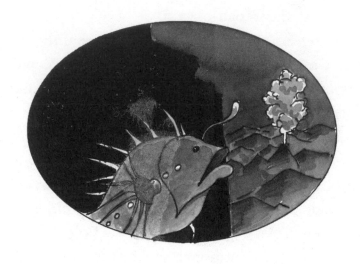

COLLECTING AND EXAMINING
SEDIMENTS ON THE OCEAN FLOOR

LET'S FIND OUT: A constant rain of all kinds of particles settles upon the sea bottom. Century after century, the particles drift down. Scientists think that the sediment carpeting much of the ocean floor is nearly half a mile thick, accumulating an inch or so every three thousand years. You might expect

120

that the sediments on the ocean floor are as smooth as a field of newly fallen snow. But that is not the case. Photographs of the ocean bottom show that deep-sea sea stars, worms, sea urchins, and other animal dwellers in the inky darkness produce mounds and burrows that churn up the top few inches. This project shows some of the ways used to explore that most mysterious of all places on Earth, the bottom of the sea.

HERE'S WHAT YOU WILL NEED: A heavy, flat weight (such as an old clothes iron); a strong cord; some plastic bags; and an assortment of sticky materials such as putty, plastic clay, or bubble gum. This is a waterside project.

HERE'S WHAT TO DO: Tie the cord firmly to the heavy weight. Put some of the sticky material on the bottom of the weight. Drop the weight into the water from a boat or a dock. When the weight hits the bottom, pull it along for a while and then haul it up. Examine the materials stuck on the bottom. Put some of the sediments in a plastic bag for more careful examination at home. If you can, use a magnifying lens or a microscope to look at the sediments for things too tiny to be seen with an unaided eye.

plastic bags

strong cord

flat weight

gum

In the early days of sea research, ocean scientists tried to retrieve sediments on the ocean floor in much the same way as in this project. They would attach wax or tallow to the bottom of a sounding line's weight and hope that some sediment would stick to it. Nowadays, deep-diving ships equipped with robot arms can gather sediment from the deepest parts of the ocean. Other ships use long hollow tubes to take core samples of the ocean floor. In more shallow areas, dredges and buckets like steam shovels pull up huge chunks of the ocean bottom.

Ocean sediments tell scientists a story of the past history of our planet Earth. For ages upon ages, material of all kinds has been filtering down to the seafloor. Once it is encased in sediments, it can be dredged up and studied by oceanographers. The sediments are a window to the past. By studying the sediments, scientists can find clues to long-dead animals and plants, extinct volcanoes, temperature changes in seawater, mineral and oil deposits, and lots more.

Can you see any bits of minerals in the sediments you collected? Try dropping the weight in different places and comparing the different kinds of sediments you pick up. Try using different kinds of sticky materials to see which work best.

Many deep-sea areas around the world are strewn with small rocks made of minerals such as manganese. These rocks, called nodules, probably formed in much the same way that you can make sugar crystals in a concentrated solution of sugar. If you would like to try forming crystals in that way, here's what to do: Dissolve ½ cup of sugar in 2 cups of warm water. Let the sugar solution stand for several days. You should begin to see bunches of sugar crystals forming as the water evaporates.

The mineral nodules on the ocean bottom are built up layer by layer, something like the layers of an onion. It is estimated that there are more than a trillion tons of manganese nodules in the Pacific Ocean alone. The nodules also contain copper, nickel, and cobalt.

The sea has many other mineral resources, ranging from oil deposits to sulfur to sand and gravel. There is no doubt that the oceans can furnish people with many of the raw materials needed by our industrial civilization.

But the future of the oceans is in doubt. For

centuries, people have dumped their wastes into the oceans without a worry that anything might harm the waters. But now we know that the waters of the ocean cannot always be counted on to clean up the mess.

Large areas of the sea have been contaminated by industrial pollution, oil spills from offshore drilling and tankers, and chemical and radioactive dumping. There is little doubt that if we continue polluting the oceans, there will be vast and dangerous changes in the environment that we cannot fully predict.

For thousands of years, the oceans were huge and threatening. In earlier times, people went to sea aware of their own helplessness in the face of the powerful waves and currents they encountered. Today, the restless ocean waters have been charted, but often are still dangerous and unpredictable.

All of us are faced with a choice: to learn to use the oceans wisely, or to continue using the waters as a vast dumping ground and hope that the ocean will take care of itself. As a young ocean scientist, you can learn to understand and appreciate the ways of the ocean. And perhaps one day you will help to determine the path that the future will take.

SUPPLIERS FOR AQUARIUM MATERIALS

(Always call or write for information and catalogue before ordering.)

Aquarium Catalog Sales
P.O. Box 86667
San Diego, CA 92109   1-800 531-7888

Aquatic Supply House
42 Hayes Street
Elmsford, NY 10523   1-800 431-8008

Daleco Mailorder
4611 Weatherside Run
Fort Wayne, IN 46804   1-219 432-4447

Discount Aquarium and Pet Supply
P.O. Box 12423
Columbus, OH 43212   1-800 433-4619

Mail Order Pet Shop
3000 O Street
Sacramento, CA 95816   1-916 452-7242

Omni Pet Products
P.O. Box 23015
Rochester, NY 14692   1-800 821-0093

Pet World Discounts
35-09 169th Street
Flushing, NY 11358   1-800 843-7387

Sanders Brine Shrimp Co.
1180 W. 4600 Street
Ogden, UT 84405   1-801 393-5027

That Fish Place
237 Centerville Road
Lancaster, PA 17603   1-800 233-3829

BOOKS FOR
READING AND RESEARCH

(Note: Some books listed may be out of print but still available in your school or public library.)

Adler, David. *Our Amazing Ocean*. Troll Associates, 1983.

Asimov, Isaac. *How Did We Find Out About Life in the Deep Sea?* Walker & Co., 1981.

Blumberg, Rhoda. *The First Travel Guide to the Bottom of the Sea*. Lothrop, Lee & Shepard Co., Inc., 1983.

Bramwell, Martin. *Oceans*. Franklin Watts, Inc., 1984.

Carson, Rachel. *The Sea Around Us* (revised edition). Oxford University Press, 1961.

Jasperson, William. *A Day in the Life of a Marine Biologist*. Little, Brown and Company, 1982.

Polking, Kirk. *Oceans of the World: Our Essential Resource*. Philomel Books (The Putnam Publishing Group, Inc.), 1983.

Poynter, Margaret, and David Collins. *Under the High Seas: New Frontiers in Oceanography*. Atheneum Publishers, 1983.

Simon, Seymour. *Tropical Saltwater Aquariums.* The Viking Press, Inc., 1976.

———. *Killer Whales.* J. B. Lippincott, 1978.

———. *From Shore to Ocean Floor: How Life Survives in the Sea.* Franklin Watts, 1973.

———. *Pets in a Jar.* The Viking Press, 1975.

INDEX